Old FAULDHOUSE

by

William F. Hendrie

Bridgend with the Co-op at the top of Store Brae. For most families the Co-op was more a way of life than simply a place to shop. Their weddings were held in the Co-op Hall, the drapery provided their babies with their first outfits, and at the other end of life the undertakers arranged their funerals. Most families were shareholders with their own Co-op number which was quoted each time they bought checks, little discs with which all purchases were paid for to ensure that they received their 'divi' (as shares of the profits were known). Members were allowed to buy on credit, but all debts had to be paid by the end of each quarter of a trading year; the final week of a quarter was known as the Lord's My Shepherd Week as it was said that God alone knew how many of the members would succeed in clearing their debts. At the end of each quarter the amount of dividend was announced and the figure affected the prosperity and morale of the whole area. A disappointing divi meant tougher times for local families. The Crofthead Co-op also had branches in other parts of the town and in neighbouring Longridge and Stoneyburn.

ACKNOWLEDGEMENTS

The author wishes to thank the many Fauldhouse folk who helped with the research
for this book including local librarian Marilyn James and her assistant Eileen
Mathieson, Meg Henderson, Marion Peek, Elizabeth Frame, Liz Wright, Tom
Farquhar, James Ford, Albert Mancini, Maurice O'Donnell, George Beuken, Teresa
Beuken, Robert Lee and William Cochrane. Special thanks also to West Lothian
Local Studies Librarian Sybil Cavanagh for her help with the selection of
photographs. Thanks also to the following for allowing reproduction of their
photographs: West Lothian Council Libraries for pages 2, 4, 15, 17–25, 27, 28, 33–41,
44, 45, 47 and the inside back cover; W.A.C. Smith for page 8; Robert Grieves for
pages 9 and 10; Mrs Faulds of Gifts & Things, Whitburn, for pages 5, 42 and 43;
Grace Carty for page 46; James McKay for page 47.

These local boys were captured on
film, probably by newspaper
photographer Joe MacLachlan, as
they enjoyed a car outing in 1954. In
the back are George Chalmers and
Jack Kerr, while in front are Charlie
Smillie and Jimmy Hamilton.

INTRODUCTION

Fauldhouse has a long history, first written mention of it occurring as long ago as 1523 when it was spelt 'Fawlhouse' meaning 'the dwelling on the unploughed land'. This accurately describes the exposed site in the south western corner of West Lothian which the town grew to occupy. At that time all of the lands in the area belonged to the Knights of the Order of St John of Jerusalem, who administered them from their headquarters eleven miles away in the village of Torphichen. In 1539 the Grand Master of the Order leased the 'Falhous' to the Waddel family, some of whose descendants still live in the village to the present day. The annual rent was to be paid in amounts of butter and cheese together with ten stirks (bullocks).

Fauldhouse was originally part of the parish of Livingston, but in 1730 it was transferred by the church authorities to the parish of Whitburn. By this time some farming was taking place in the area, but its height above sea level combined with its remoteness made it a difficult area to cultivate and it was not until its rural calm was suddenly changed to one of industrial bustle that the town began to grow and prosper.

This dramatic change in its fortunes occurred in 1790 when the Wilsontown Iron Company from nearby Lanarkshire began to dig for coal, and the influx of miners and their large families brought a sudden increase in population to 1,330. There was an even greater boost about half a century later when in 1845 geologists discovered a valuable bed of slatey ironstone. This rich find was quickly developed by Messrs Holdsworth Ltd of Coltness, who already had ironworks in Lanarkshire, and by the Shotts Iron Company.

Both companies sank several small pits and installed steam pumping engines to raise the ironstone to the surface. The ore was then loaded into railway wagons and transported a short distance away from the pits. There it was dumped in piles and covered over with tons of earth or ashes before being set ablaze to obtain pure iron by the process of calcination. The burning of the ironstone caused billowing yellow clouds of sulphurous smoke to spiral heavenward, leading to a contemporary description of Fauldhouse as being 'like a living Hell on Earth!'. This hellish appearance was added to by the fact that the sulphur killed off all the grass, shrubs and bushes in the area. The evil smelling sulphur not only caught the breath but also polluted the nearby River Almond and the Breich Burn to such an extent that no fish could live in either of these waters. It was necessary to burn one thousand tons of ironstone to produce a mere sixty tons of iron. Every ton of iron, however, was worth money and it was the value of this product and the demand for it which resulted in the railway reaching Fauldhouse in the 1840s, long before there were rail links to many larger Scottish towns.

The coming of the railway made Fauldhouse less isolated and one benefit was that the brightest of the local boys and girls could travel by train to obtain secondary education at Bathgate Academy. Primary education was provided by the original parish school at Crofthead and at the elementary school provided by the other large local employer, British Industrial Sands, for children of their workers at Levenseat Quarry. When most Fauldhouse boys left school, however, it was to work in the pits or the ironworks. (In 1873 new restrictions introduced by the Mines Act meant that six lads who had already started work had to be readmitted to school until officially old enough to leave.) Fauldhouse did not obtain its own secondary school until the School Board built the premises at Crofthead in 1901 which later became known as Fauldhouse Junior Secondary.

The name 'Fauldhouse' was originally used only to describe one of the many clusters of miners' rows which were hurriedly built by the colliery owners to house the ever-increasing numbers of miners and their families attracted to the area by the work provided by the pits. Around 1870, however, it became the accepted title for the town which by then also embraced the hamlets of Benthead, Crofthead, Drybridge, Gowanbrae, Greenburn and Shepherdshill or Sheephousehill as it became known. Fauldhouse grew so rapidly that the 1871 census recorded a population of 3,200, making it the third largest town in West Lothian – only Bathgate and Bo'ness were larger. Twenty years later Fauldhouse had grown further still to 3,467 residents. A century later, however, while the populations of Bathgate and Bo'ness had both grown to over 14,000, the population of Fauldhouse was only 4,766; regarded by outsiders as somewhat remote, it has not succeeded in attracting the large housing developments of the other towns.

The comparatively isolated position of Fauldhouse, however, has made it a ruggedly independent little community. Much of this community spirit continues to flourish, showing itself through support for many organisations ranging from the town's brass band to its Scottish Junior Cup-winning football team, its bowling club, its eighteen hole golf course and the famous Victoria Cricket Club, as well as its annual children's gala day.

Many of these Fauldhouse institutions, as well as its pubs, shops and businesses of former years, are featured in this book, which hopefully will interest not only long time residents, but also the new families who have happily chosen to make this township the place they call home.

Main Street, looking east, *c.* 1906. The long low line of cottages, known locally as Garibaldi Row, still stands on the corner of Bridge Street, unlike the premises of the Fauldhouse Co-op on the Store Brae whose roof rises behind them in the background. Fauldhouse must have been a smoky town because as a mining community all of its homes were heated by open coal fires. Indeed, many miners received an allowance of coal to supplement their meagre wages. The two-storey block on the right belonged originally to the Commercial Bank and is now a branch of the Royal Bank of Scotland, which took it over. Known as the Bank House, the bank manager, or bank agent as the position was originally known, for many years lived directly above the office. This custom was aimed at making customers feel that their money was more secure. 100 years ago the cottage on the left, now John Brannan's butcher's, was occupied by Baldy Brown's shoe and boot shop.

4

Main Street, looking west, *c.* 1925. Behind the woman on the left is Garibaldi Row and the bank building. The building on the immediate right is Greenhill which was built in 1903 and was originally a private home. It took its name from the fact that it was built from the stones of the then recently demolished Greenhill School at Greenburn. Latterly, it became the offices of a local firm of solicitors and now lies disused. Before the Junior Secondary School was built, Fauldhouse had three smaller schools at Crofthead, at the top of the Store Brae where the Co-op later had its dairy premises, and Greenhill School which was run by the Dixon Company for the education of its miners' children. Another of Main Street's well-known landmarks is Stark's pub, the Heather Bell Inn. The pub probably acquired this name because East Benhar Heatherbell football club played its matches in a field behind it. The single-storey building in the middle of the picture was formerly a butcher's shop. Cattle and sheep used to be driven along Main Street and through an adjacent close to the slaughterhouse behind the shop.

West End & Caledonian Hotel, Fauldhouse.

Since the 1840s, Fauldhouse had been well-served by railways with lines belonging to two different companies passing through the town. The Caledonian Hotel, the building in the centre of the picture with the flagpole, was conveniently situated for passengers arriving at the town's North Station which had been opened a short distance further to the west in 1867 by the Caledonian Railway Company.

WEST END FAULDHOUSE

The town originally had another railway station at Crofthead which had been opened in 1846 by the Wilsontown, Morningside and Coltness Railway Company. With two passenger stations, Fauldhouse was one of the best served towns in West Lothian for rail links. Travel times were one hour to both Glasgow Central and Edinburgh Princes Street, half an hour to Wishaw, twenty minutes to Bathgate, and eight minutes to Shotts. There were also connections from Fauldhouse to Motherwell, Coatbridge and Bellshill. On the left are miners' rows and it was houses such as these that made up the bulk of Fauldhouse's homes. By 1900 there were almost 200 houses in the village, housing a population of over 700 miners and their families. Other rows included Red Row, Slate Row, Post Office Row, School Row, Station Row, Fallas Row, Garibaldi Row and the row always known simply as the Den.

This picture of Fauldhouse North Station shows the arrival of the 3.44 p.m. service from Edinburgh Princes Street to Glasgow Central, drawn by a class 4, 2-6-4T engine, no. 42273. The station buildings have long been demolished and replaced by a plastic covered shelter and services are now drawn by diesel multiple units rather than steam locomotives. However, the trains still provide an important transport link for the people of Fauldhouse and the surrounding area.

Faced with competition from the bus companies which established themselves in the early decades of the twentieth century, the railways no longer enjoyed the monopoly on public transport. This situated meant that Fauldhouse could no longer support two stations and Crofthead was closed in 1930. This Daimler bus belonged to the local bus operator, John Beuken, whose main service connected Shotts, Fauldhouse and Bathgate. Beuken's was one of the earliest bus fleets in West Lothian and his first buses were twelve seaters with running boards stretching the length of both sides.

A brand new Bean bus at Beuken's East End Garage, 1929. The firm was awarded a public service vehicle licence to operate the bus service from Shotts to Bathgate. This put them in direct competition with the S.M.T. bus company and there are many stories of the buses of the two companies battling to win the race to pick up customers along the route through Fauldhouse. In 1931 Beuken was taken over by the S.M.T. who acquired all of the firm's eight assorted buses, including three Beans. Many years later, however, the Beukens re-entered the coach trade as private hirers running much more modern Bedford 33-seater buses. The young conductor in the picture, looking on as the driver fills the fuel tank, is John Mills who later became an electrician in the pits.

West End, Fauldhouse.

During its lifetime the Caledonian Hotel survived three major fires but it no longer dispenses hospitality as it has now been converted into private apartments. In 1896 a meeting was held in the hotel to found the local golf club. Beyond the hotel on the left is the row known as Portland Terrace, remembered nowadays in the name Portland Place. A coal train is crossing the bridge in the background.

WESTEND, FAULDHOUSE

The many pedestrians in this view suggest that it may have been taken on the occasion of some special summer event in the town. Could it perhaps have been early in the morning of one of the town's first gala days? The railway used to cross the street at road level but after St John the Baptist Primary School was opened in 1916 the viaduct was erected to improve safety.

DRILL HOUSE & BAILLIE INSTITUTE, FAULDHOUSE.

On the immediate right is the Drill House where the local Volunteers, an early version of the Home Guard, practised their shooting in its long narrow rifle range. Beside the Drill House is the Miners' Institute and the original Baillie Institute which are now integrated with each other. The Baillie Institute was gifted to the town by the Baillie family, local coal mine owners who lived at Polkemmet House after which the country park is named. The Fauldhouse building with its hall, meeting rooms, reading room and library was one of five similar institutes which they established in other West Lothian towns. The Miners' Institute Welfare Hall is a place of happy memories for many Fauldhouse folk as it was there that they did their courting at the regular weekly Saturday night dances. The town's war memorial is also situated here.

The photographer caught the attention of these young residents of Bridge Street when he took this view along it towards Main Street during the early 1900s. The Masonic Lodge can be seen on the left. It still occupies this site but its hall has been greatly enlarged. Businesses in Bridge Street, or Dry Bridge Street as it was originally known, have included Mrs Salmond's bakery, Chalmers the ironmongers, James Grieve the licensed grocer, Miss Margaret Graham's shoe shop which later belonged to Mrs Montgomery, and a branch of the Co-op.

Bridge Street, Fauldhouse.

Bridge St, Fauldhouse.

A well-known Fauldhouse drinking howf, known latterly as the Running Dog, stands out on the left in this view of Bridge Street. The flight of outside stairs on the left of the building led to the publican's house which was directly above the pub. For many years the licensee was Mr McCathie. In the past, Fauldhouse's licensed premises benefited greatly from Scotland's former strict Sunday drink laws. These insisted that to be served alcohol on the Sabbath a customer had to be what was described in legal terms as a bonafide traveller. To qualify as such a customer had to show that he had travelled more than two miles and Fauldhouse was ideally situated to attract this trade from Shotts and other neighbouring towns and villages. This photograph was published and sold as a picture postcard by Mrs Murray who had a small shop in Main Street.

The Fallas Bridge,
& Post Office Brae,
Fauldhouse.

The Post Office was housed in the small cottage on the right which still stands on the brae at the Fallas. It is situated opposite where the gates of the old Manse used to stand but like the house these have long since disappeared. This was the second post office in Fauldhouse. The first was opened at Greenburn in 1849 and closed at the beginning of the 1870s. It was when it reopened at the cottage at the Fallas Bridge that mail was for the first time hand-franked with the name Fauldhouse. The thick clump of trees on the right later became the site of the Palace Theatre. It originally staged variety acts, but when silent films became popular in the 1920s it was quickly adapted to be able to show them, accompanied by well-known local pianist, Meg Clark. The Mancini family, Italian immigrants who came to the town in the 1890s and who ran a nearby ice-cream and fish and chip shop, later renamed their premises the Palace Cafe after the theatre.

THE FALLAS, FAULDHOUSE.

Many of the patrons of the Palace Theatre and Mancini's cafe lived nearby in the crowded Fallas Rows. This picture of the miners' rows there was taken from the mineral railway bridge at the west end. The two-storey building set back on the left was originally the Dixon Coal Company's store, which the Co-op was built to challenge. The Dixon store was often known as the truck shop from the fact that the miners and their wives were allowed to obtain goods which they desperately needed on credit which was known as 'truck'. The evil of the truck system was that by ensuring their miners were in debt to them, Dixon's and other companies like it prevented the men from leaving their employment or even threatening to go on strike. The shop was later operated by Gavin Thomson. By the First World War the town had electric power as the poles show, but at that time the houses did not have piped water and supplies had to be fetched from stand pipes in the street.

A water stand pipe in front of Castle Row, East Benhar, *c.* 1920. The families who inhabited these red brick rows on the outskirts of Fauldhouse had to fetch their water from these and in the days before pithead baths were provided this could be a considerable amount as every miner expected his wife to have a tin bath ready for him when he arrived home from his shift. Dry privies were situated outdoors in the back gardens. Despite the lack of such basic facilities, the miners' wives took great pride in their two-roomed homes. The most important feature of the livingroom was the iron range for heating and cooking which was kept immaculately black leaded, a task which took several hours each week. Castle Row was built by the Benhar Coal Company after it developed a colliery nearby during the 1860s. In 1906 the pit and its accompanying rows was taken over by a rival company, Barr and Thornton, who continued to operate it until it closed in 1929 throwing its miners out of work. Abandoned by the mine company, the rows rapidly deteriorated and in 1932 West Lothian County Council decided to move the remaining families to new houses which it had erected in Fauldhouse.

Braehead Colliery, pictured here in the 1930s, was operated by Barr and Thornton. It was closed in 1944 and two years later the area suffered a further blow when the Knowes Colliery was closed after a series of disputes and strikes by the miners. They sent a deputation to London to lobby the new Labour government's Minister of Fuel and Power, Emmanuel Shinwell, to persuade him to keep it open. They hoped for a sympathetic hearing from the legendary 'Manny' because they had helped send him to Westminster as M.P. for West Lothian, but he declined to see them and the closure went ahead. All trace of these and Fauldhouse's many other pits has long since vanished, but before all of the colliery buildings were demolished one of them became home to the Price family whose patriarch was regarded as king of the Scottish travelling folk. When he died in the 1960s, the local police helped communicate with other travelling families all over Scotland and the north of England and hundreds of them travelled to Fauldhouse for the funeral. After it they gathered round to watch as his van was set alight and burnt as tradition demanded.

As well as the many collieries, Fauldhouse also had a flourishing brick works which was situated on the outskirts of the town at East Benhar. In addition to its tall smoke stacks, its two beehive shaped kilns in which the clay bricks were baked can also be seen on the left.

Millions of bricks were required during the 1930s for the construction of local authority council housing. These modern new homes with their running water and mains supply of electricity and gas revolutionised the Scottish way of life and nowhere more so than in Fauldhouse, where the miners' rows were demolished to make way for these new houses at Lanrigg Road, Victoria Road and Barton Terrace.

Two brickies taking a break from work on these council houses in Lanrigg Road. The tenants of these new homes, mostly from the town's miners' rows, paid weekly rents. One of the largest and best known families in Fauldhouse were the McSherrys and it was in a house like these that their mother Sal, who was widowed while still a young woman, single-handedly raised her fifteen children. She lived in the town until 1999, when she passed away within weeks of reaching her 100th birthday. Her family honoured her memory by returning from many parts of the world to hold a Millennium reunion in their home town.

Completed houses awaiting occupation when the photographer took this picture of the Lanrigg area of the town in the early 1930s. Further new housing, including high flats, was built in Fauldhouse in the 1950s by the Scottish Special Housing Association to accommodate Glasgow overspill families. The council houses and the S.S.H.A. houses ranged in size from three to five apartment homes each equipped with modern bathrooms and kitchens and with good cupboard capacity.

Many of the families who moved into new homes in Fauldhouse purchased furniture, linoleum and carpets from Casey's shop opposite the Square at Bridgend. It also had a drapery department selling clothes for all of the family in the days when Fauldhouse was much more self-sufficient and shopping expeditions to Glasgow or Bathgate were rare treats reserved for the summer holidays or Christmas. In addition to selling clothing, furniture and bedding, Casey's also operated a licensed pawnbroker business. This enabled local people who were short of money to deposit belongings such as jewellery and watches and receive cash for them, before hopefully recovering them on pay day by paying back the sum borrowed (with interest added, of course). Casey's store is now occupied by Vantage Chemists. The shed on the right was the garage for the local taxi which can be glimpsed through the open door. In the days before the N.H.S., Mrs Casey also looked after the local ambulance; one of the best known of its drivers was Bobby Melrose.

A view of the Square from around 1950, pre-dating the construction of the Community Centre, the Scotmid Co-operative supermarket, newsagents and pharmacy, the Public Library and the premises of St John the Baptist primary school. The church is St Andrew's which belongs to the Church of Scotland. In the seventeenth century, Fauldhouse had strong links with the Covenanter's movement and conventicles – open air services organised in conditions of top secrecy – were often held on the surrounding moors which allowed worshippers plenty of warning if government redcoat dragoons approached. The prominent Covenanter, Richard Cameron, who was killed by the government troops at Airds Moss near Strathaven, preached his last sermon at Fauldhouse and a stone cairn to mark his memory was erected in the woods near the town. Its ruined remains still stand.

The old Fauldhouse Junior Secondary School still stands in Sheephousehill, but has been converted into Crofthead House Nursing Home. The school was built in 1901 to cope with the rapidly increasing number of children in the town. Many older residents will remember its headmasters: Mr MacDonald, John Lyle who was in charge between 1934 and 1963, Mr Orr, and finally, Hamish Miller. In 1967 the school became Crofthead Primary and local children had to travel to the secondary school in Whitburn. The stone wall surrounding the school playground in this photograph was later replaced by iron railings and the wrought iron gates were locked after the morning bell had rung. Pupils who arrived late had to wait to be admitted by the janitor who escorted them to the headmaster's room to ensure there was no escape from punishment with the thick leather tawse whose strokes Fauldhouse children called 'palmies' as they were administered to the outstretched, upturned palms of their hands.

A class of six year olds with their teacher, Miss Chalmers, photographed in 1923 at the 'Big Public' (the local nickname for the building also occupied by Junior Secondary pupils). Fauldhouse Infant School also existed at this period and its Victorian premises still stand, now incorporated into the modern Falla Hill Primary School which was officially opened in 1975. In February 2000 the pupils marked the new Millennium by staging a special exhibition about the town's past. It came as a huge surprise to older Fauldhouse residents when many of the children admitted that they had never previously seen a lump of coal. Part of the display was devoted to the school's own history and the boys and girls were particularly interested in the old fashioned high desk and tall wooden chair on which the teacher used to sit in order to see any misdeeds going on in the class. These were promptly punished by a stroke of the Lochgelly tawse, which to the horror of the modern youngsters was also prominently displayed (although any fear of actual chastisement with it disappeared with the abolition of corporal punishment in 1981).

The school had 'skailed' (dismissed) in this photograph and pupils rushed along the street past the horse-drawn cart in the middle of the road, happy to be out of class. A particularly popular place with the boys and girls was the little shop on the corner of Quarry Road (on the right) which acted as the school tuck shop and was always well-stocked with chocolate bars and sweeties including bull's eyes, dolly mixtures and liquorice-all-sorts. Meg Henderson recalls that if her class had been very well-behaved all week her teacher, Miss Nelson, sent one of the pupils across to the shop to buy butternuts with which to reward them all before they went home on Friday afternoons. The hill in the background was known locally as Doctor's Brae as it led up to the homes and surgeries of the well-known local general practitioners, Dr Ogilvie and Dr Gilchrist. Behind the trees on the left of the brae was the home of maths teacher Miss Marion Muir, who only had a short walk each morning from her house to reach her classroom in the Junior Secondary School.

SHEEPHOUSE HILL, FAULDHOUSE.

More children photographed further along from the school in Sheephousehill. The high roof of the school is visible in the background.

Sheephousehill, Fauldhouse.

Children often played safely in the middle of Sheephousehill in the days when there was very little road traffic apart from horse-drawn carts. The street was more often crossed by steam engines pulling long rows of coal wagons and the lines of one of the level crossings can be seen in the foreground. There were two branch railways, one to Eastfield and the other to Greenburn. The Eastfield route also had two level crossings in Longridge Road. It crossed Sheephousehill at Beuken's Garage and served the old coal pit which was originally situated behind it. The line then crossed Eastfield Road and passed behind the school buildings before reaching the ironstone mine which was near the cricket ground. It then continued over Longridge Road and ended at the coal pit near the School Rows. It is still possible to stroll along the routes of many railway lines and this particular line is one of the most pleasant walks in the Fauldhouse area.

In this view of Sheephousehill, looking towards Doctor's Brae, the old Esso petrol pump at Beuken's Garage is on the left. The garage was later relocated further along Sheephouse Road before eventually being resited again to the present site where it still does business. Apart from their bus services, the Beukens also operated a fleet of taxis and a road haulage business. Amongst the loads which they carried were the organically grown products from their own greenhouses: tomatoes and cucumbers in summer and tulips in winter. The enterprising family also produced firelighters from black peat. This product was gathered from the moors around Fauldhouse then dipped in bitumen which was melted in a boiler in the yard. Grandfather of the family, John Beuken, was also involved in the development of the Benhar Moss Litter Company which had a factory in Fauldhouse and its products were used as fuel for heating, in horticulture and in the production of malt whisky. A second firm, the Peat Company, was also developed further afield in the North of England, but the Beukens always kept Fauldhouse as their base and several members of the family still live in the town.

BOWLING GREEN FAULDHOUSE.

Fauldhouse has always been well-supplied with sports facilities, including the bowling green whose background rows of trees have long ago been replaced by lines of houses. A golf club was established in Fauldhouse in 1896. The first golf course at Eastfield had only six holes, but the present one, which was re-established in 1953, has the full eighteen. When its new clubhouse was erected in 1966 it cost £19,000. Athletics was also popular and, in boxing, Johnny Smillie, twice Amateur Boxing Association flyweight champion, and British heavyweight champion John Fisher, were both local heroes who reached the top in their sport.

Fauldhouse has always been one of Scotland's cricketing strongholds, and its cricket club is the oldest in West Lothian and the third oldest in Scotland. Its Victoria club (probably named after the local pit of that name) was founded in 1855 and was originally known as Crofthead Victoria after the local colliery. Matches were originally played on a pitch at Greenburn and fixtures were later moved to Station Park, a site now occupied by the government civil defence store. The club obtained its present site in 1900 with the help of local farmer Jackie Wyper, whose daughter later presented it with a trophy which is still played for. The first match was played at it two years later. The boys in this young eleven represented Fauldhouse Junior Secondary School in the early 1950s. In the background is the school's covered shed where pupils sheltered during playtimes on wet and windy days. Often the scene of playground games such as tig, it was also the venue for closely contested conker championships in autumn and fiercely fought games of marbles when the warmer days of spring arrived. One feature whose disappearance no one mourns, however, were the outside toilets which can be glimpsed in the corner beyond the shed.

Football has always been the most popular of all school sports and this photograph shows the Fauldhouse Junior Secondary School's First Eleven during the 1952-53 season. For many of the lads their ambition was to go on to play for Fauldhouse United, the town's junior team which has always had a strong reputation in Scottish football. United's finest hour came at the end of the 1945-46 season when they defeated Arthurlie in the final of the Scottish Junior Cup by two goals to nil. On their way to the final, they also defeated Blantyre Victoria before a record breaking crowd of 10,000 spectators which provided them with support which many modern First Division sides can only envy. In that triumphant season the team played 45 games in a row without a single defeat and won four other major trophies.

In 1950 these were the boys who played in the Primary 6-7 team at St John the Baptist School. They are, back row: Jim Clupp, Robert Campbell, Eddie Watson, Jim Timmins, Hugh Timmins and John McSherry; front row: Burns (first name unknown), James McIlduff, Andy Mooney, John Timmins and Derek Timmins. John Timmins went on to play for a rather more famous team – Manchester United! – and several of his school mates also went on to play for other professional sides.

Around the same year the St John the Baptist Primary School netball team consisted of, back row: Rose Boyle, Mary Whelan, Klomovitch (first name unknown) and Rose Scally; front row: Helen Riley, Jane Thomas and Anne Scott with their teachers and team coaches, Mrs Watson on the left and Miss Clark (later Mrs Carlin) on the right.

During their school years, the ambition of many local girls was to be chosen to be the town's gala – or Fallas – queen. Jessie Brown – photographed here in the early 1920s – was the earliest of the gala queens. The sceptre she is holding was the queen's symbol of office while her throne was actually an antique wooden chair loaned by a Mrs Francis.

Queen Jane Carty, or Jeannie as she was known to her family, was crowned in 1925 and this portrait of her was taken by local photographer Mr K. Cartwight. She is wearing the same costume as Jessie.

The annual summer gala day, held on a Saturday in June, is always a highlight for the town and many expatriates return faithfully each year to the town to watch the coronation ceremony. The crowning of the town's queen still takes place with the same pomp and ceremony as at this gala in the late 1940s although at that time postwar rationing meant that costumes and decorations could not be bought new each year. Instead, costumes were re-used from year to year and the gala day committee even lifted carpets from the floors of their own homes to deck out the coronation platform.

In 1950 the girl chosen to be gala queen was May Cook who is pictured here accompanied by her champion and flanked by the flower girls of her royal retinue. This photograph was taken by local newspaper photographer Joe MacLachlan whose work appeared each week in the *West Lothian Courier*. Joe also covered all of the home games played by Fauldhouse United of whom he was an especially keen supporter as they were trained by another member of the MacLachlan family, the famous Dixie.

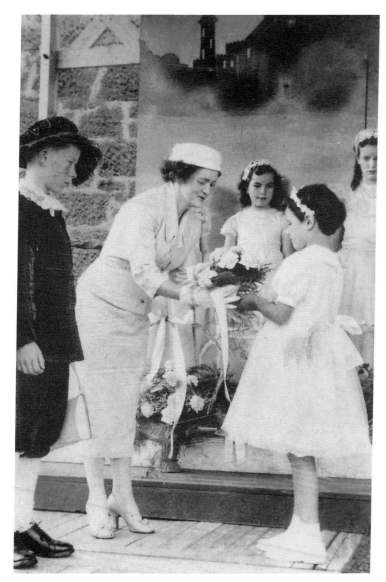

After her coronation the queen always makes her royal progress through the large crowds who have turned out to see her crowned. For well over a century Fauldhouse has been famed for the excellence of its brass band and its rousing playing always contributes to the atmosphere of gala day.

Once her duties are completed at the gala the local lady who has been honoured to crown the queen is always presented with a bouquet of flowers, as seen in this photograph from the 1950s.

A 1930s photograph of the gala procession snaking its way down the Store Brae and past the Drybrig. In 1937 the Co-operative Society took over the running of the gala day and they were able to obtain a horse-drawn landau from Edinburgh on which the queens could ride to their crowning ceremonies. The horse and carriage always arrived the night before the procession and was looked after by Mr Gordon, who was later amongst the tenants at Blackfaulds Court.

Mrs Bishop's Highland dance classes were a popular feature of Fauldhouse life during the 1950s when this photograph and the one on the next page were taken by Joe MacLachlan. The smiling lassie in the middle of the back row is Margaret Macintosh and the piper is believed to be a Mr Baillie.

The girls who attended Mrs Bishop's dance classes often performed at concerts at places as varied as Scottish Woman's Institute parties and Shotts Prison. As well as the traditional Highland dances such as the fling and swords, the younger girls also performed tap and other routines. The girls in the picture include Christine Middleton and Sandra Boyce, who is understood to have later emigrated to Canada.

A few years earlier in the 1940s, a piano accordionist entertained these Fauldhouse folk who took part in this occasion for smart dress – a wedding or an outing perhaps? Can any readers identify what it was or any of the faces in the picture?

Photographed during the 1950s, members of Crofthead Co-operative Women's Guild are seen here marking a special occasion with the cutting of a cake. The ceremony took place in the Co-op Hall on the first floor of the society's premises at the top of the Store Brae and the large iced and decorated cake may well have been baked in the adjoining Co-op bakery.

In 1953 the coronation of Queen Elizabeth was marked in Fauldhouse by the presentation of commemorative postage stamps to the town's children of pre-school age. On that warm June day the stamps were handed over to the youngsters by the Rev. Peter Davidson, minister of Fauldhouse United Free Church. He was later called to a large church in Aberdeen and his church in Fauldhouse has long since been demolished (its spire can be seen to the right of the Co-op building on the front cover). Other people in this picture, taken outside the Miners' Institute Hall in Bridge Street, include Bessie Easton with her baby son Bill in her arms, Nan Woods who is bending down, Grace Carty with her wee boy Brian, Johnny Proven, Mary Connell, Mary Mooney, Mr Nielson, Henry Brown and Kate Muir who is at the back on the right.

These East Benhar miners posed for the cameraman outside the local Welfare Hall. They are wearing their Sunday best clothes and the style of their caps suggests they were probably photographed around the year 1930. These large flat caps were nicknamed 'doo landers', a name derived from one of the miners' favourite hobbies, breeding racing pigeons. They took great pride in their birds which were kept in wooden lofts behind the rows and often considerable amounts of money were gambled on the result of a race. Fauldhouse still has a club for pigeon fanciers with premises in Main Street. Back row: Sam Hutchison, Davie Park, Robert MacMillan and Paddy McKay; middle row: Wee Sammy Hutchison and Tosh Clark; front row: Davie Lawrence, Unknown, Johnny Thomson and Speedie Leach.

Although often thought of as a gritty industrial town, Fauldhouse has also had its local beauty spots. This is how Leadloch Avenue looked around the year 1910. Farms around Fauldhouse included one at the Fallas whose fields have long disappeared as a result of housing developments, but others with a long history still exist at Holehouseburn, Crofthead and Croftfoot. The latter, which is situated to the south of the town near the Breich Burn, was originally a typical Scottish long house with the farm beasts accommodated at one end of the building while the farmer and his family lived at the other end.

A special childhood favourite of past generations was this peaceful spot where stepping stones led across the Breich Burn or the Breichie as it was always known. Further along the course of the river was Happy Valley where ferns were often gathered to decorate arches and house frontages on the town's annual gala day.